Live with In*ten*tion

Ten Steps to Creating the Life of Your Dreams

"*Live with intention. Walk to the edge.*
Listen hard. Practice wellness.
Play with abandon.
Laugh.
Choose with no regret. Continue to learn.
Appreciate your friends. Do what you love.
Love as if this is all there is."

—*Mary Anne Radmacher*

Live with Intention

Ten Steps to Creating the Life of Your Dreams

Adair Cates

Published by:
Synergy Shift LLC
28 White Pine Drive, Asheville, NC 28805
828-413-4019
email: adair@synergyshift.com
www.adaircates.com • www.synergyshift.com

ISBN: 978-0-9814633-0-8

Live with Intention

Ten Steps to Creating the Life of Your Dreams

Acknowledgements

First and foremost, I thank my wonderful husband, Chris, who came up with the idea of putting this book together. Thank you for your constant support and encouragement. You have been with me every step of the way and are a big part of my success. Our commitment to move together confidently in the direction of our dreams will continue to lead to unlimited success for both of us and a lifelong relationship of love, joy and understanding.

Also, I thank my Mom, who first introduced me to the secret. If it weren't for you, I wouldn't have bought Rhonda Byrne's book and DVD, *The Secret*. The information from those two sources changed my life and caused a sleeping tiger inside of me to awaken. Thanks, Mom, for always being such an amazing person and teacher. Thanks also to all of my family and friends who believed in me and supported me along the way.

I thank my students who have been open to receiving my messages and teachings. From my students at Blue Ridge Community College to those in my Master Mind groups, you are what keep me going. A teacher can't teach if the students aren't there to listen. My reason for being on the planet is to empower and inspire others, so without you as my students, I would be unable to live out my life purpose.

Thank you to Shelley Lieber for believing in this project and helping me see it through to completion. Serendipity (or the Law of Attraction!) certainly brought you into my life at the perfect time.

I also thank Jack Canfield for his writings and teachings. You have been a true inspiration to me and a big influence in the creation and writing of this book. I also thank Lee Caldwell of Jack Canfield's coaching program for encouraging me to write daily to finish my book.

Thanks to all of these very influential people who I have read, seen and listened to and learned a wealth of knowledge from: Bob Proctor, Esther and Jerry Hicks, T. Harv Eker, Dan Millman, Deepak Chopra and Brian Biro.

Finally, thanks to Dr. Wayne Dyer. A CD from your *Inner Wisdom* library that I listened to over and over again in the car as I drove to and from my old job gave me the courage to quit teaching Spanish and to pursue my passion. You introduced new consciousness to me through materials like *The Power of Intention* in ways that were so subtle and gentle, yet so powerful. Thanks for being such an amazing spiritual master.

Contents

Adair Cates

Introduction

Are you getting the results you want in all areas of your life? How are your finances, relationships and health? How much leisure time do you have? What are you doing to serve others? If you stayed on the path that you're on now, where do you think you would end up?

If you're like most people, chances are you want better results in your life. Well, you've come to the right place! Congratulations on taking the first step toward creating the life you've always dreamed of. This book will show you how writing down your intentions (what you want for yourself) and visualizing them for at least ten minutes a day will lead to results you never thought possible.

What does it mean to live with intention?

Living with intention means living with passion and purpose. It means knowing what you want out of life and working in harmony with the universe to make it happen. Living with intention means being inspired by a thought or an idea and believing in it and yourself enough to see it through to manifestation.

Intention is inner power and faith that everything you need will show up at the perfect time. In his book, *The Power of Intention,* Dr. Wayne Dyer says, "Intention is not something you do but rather a force that exists in the universe as an invisible field of energy—a power that can carry us."

The intentions you write and study in this book are like magnets that work in accordance with the Law of Attraction, which states that like attracts like. Whatever you choose to call into existence is yours, because the Law of Attraction is obedient. Philosopher, author and success coach Bob Proctor says in Rhonda Byrne's book, *The Secret,* "If you see it in your mind, you're going to hold it in your hand."

You have two choices in life: to take the circumstances that life gives you, or to create your own. If you choose the latter, which you obviously have since you bought this book, the process of living with intention is simple:

- Let go of old programming

- Feel good and remain in a constant state of gratitude

- Live "on purpose"

- Study and visualize your intentions for ten minutes a day, feeling them as already complete

- Believe your intentions are possible

- Detach from outcomes

- Act when appropriate

- Celebrate your successes

Sit back and watch your intentions manifest before your eyes! When you decide what you want, you send a message out to the universe and the universe, in turn, responds to your request. The following story about the power of intention in my life is a perfect example.

The power of intention in my life

Before writing this book, I had my own book of intentions. I got the idea from *The Success Principles* by Jack Canfield. In his book, Canfield suggests writing down your goals and studying them each day. Also, he suggests using visual aids to form clearer images of the goals.

After spending hours cutting out magazine pictures and neatly writing down my intentions on 4x6 note cards per Canfield's suggestions, I realized that I had done them incorrectly. I had not written them in complete, expressive, present-tense sentences and had not been very specific.

A bit disappointed, I went back through the cards and attempted to re-write them. I added some descriptive adjectives and marked out the verbs to change them to the present tense, but they ended up looking like a big mess. Instead of getting discouraged, I put them away and intended to come up with a viable solution or to make new ones.

One afternoon, when my husband, Chris, and I were driving in the car and having one of our visionary conversations, he said, "Have you ever thought about creating a book of your intentions?"

I said, "No, but that's a great idea. And if I make one for myself, why couldn't I make one for other people?"

Not only had I gotten an awesome solution to my messy cards, but I also had a book idea! When I got home that day, I sat down at my computer and wrote my book of intentions.

I knew I would be seeing Jack Canfield speak in Toronto in less than a week, so I hurriedly copied and bound my intentions into a book and officially made showing him my fabulous idea one of my intentions. From that point forward, I visualized the meeting I would have with him.

Though this goal seemed very lofty, I put lots of energy into it and believed it was possible. After all, I had done a lot of reading and studying on setting intentions, but I had never tested out my new knowledge on such a grand scale.

The day before the conference in Toronto, as my mom and I were sitting in the hotel lobby, Jack Canfield walked in the main entrance! He was alone, and I knew this was my chance to make my intention come true.

I got up quickly, book in hand, and proceeded to have the exact conversation with him that I had played out in my head. No kidding! It was a life-changing moment, and from that point on, I have recognized the power I have to create my life.

I sent Jack Canfield a very preliminary copy of my book and

though nothing further happened at that point, his recognizing its innovativeness and quality made me feel more compelled to make it happen.

You, too, can harness the power of intention through the use of this book. What started out as my personal book grew from merely an intention into a creation. I hope that you use it as I have to manifest the life you've always dreamed of.

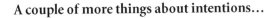
check this one out too!

A couple of more things about intentions...

I thought I was finished with the manuscript of this book until I read Deepak's Chopra's book, *The Spontaneous Fulfillment of Desire*. It is a fascinating book that I highly recommend. From it, I learned a few more essentials about setting intentions and creating your life:

- The ultimate goal of all intentions is happiness and fulfillment

- Intentions come from and must be aligned with the universal domain

- Attachment to the outcome of your intentions will only block their realization

The ultimate goal of all intentions is happiness and fulfillment. Even though one of your intentions is to own a home on the beach in Maui, if you keep asking yourself, "What is my true intention?" the core of it is happiness and fulfillment. Perhaps a home in Maui would be a retreat where you could escape to read and write and get in touch with your higher self, or maybe it is a place to meet your family for a two-week vacation. Though many of our intentions are material, they are ultimately spiritual. When setting your intentions, remember that their true purpose is to create more love, joy, peace and harmony in your life and in the world.

Chopra said, "In the beginning your intentions may be all about 'self' and the little details of what you want to happen in your life. But eventually you will realize that the goal is fulfillment at all levels, not just the personal or ego level."

No matter what your intention is, you must recognize that it comes from, and therefore must be aligned with, the universal domain. This means that the manifestation of your intention has to be a result that is harmonious not only with you, but also with the universe.

After you have written your intentions, it is important to pay attention to them, but it is also important to let them go. You must not be concerned with how, or if, your intentions will materialize, or how long it might take. Intentions cannot be forced or pushed but instead must flow smoothly from you and out into the universe.

I experienced the importance of detachment firsthand not too long ago. In the very beginning stages of my career as a motivational speaker, trainer and coach, I proposed a contract to coach nine retail store managers. The regional manager accepted the proposal but had to get approval for funding from the parent company.

This big-dollar contract was going to prove to my doubting

friends, family and former colleagues that I was going to make it in my new career. As I waited for the approval, I became obsessed about all the things I could do with the money and how I couldn't wait to tell everyone about my big break. I couldn't stop talking and thinking about the contract and actually slowed down other business activities just knowing that I was going to get it and wouldn't have much time for other clients.

Well, after two weeks waiting neurotically for an answer, I got an email letting me know that the contract request had not gone through. I was devastated! I cried and even got angry, not understanding why, if I had wanted it so badly, I hadn't gotten the contract.

After a hike in nature to refocus my energy, I looked back on the situation and saw how I had become attached to the outcome. I was more focused on the money and proving myself to others than I was on my true reason for working in this field: to inspire, empower and serve others. I vowed not to repeat my mistake.

Only days after this temporary defeat, I got my first coaching client in a very opposite manner. I enthusiastically presented him with the advantages of personal coaching and intended to have him as my first client. I felt confident that I had done everything I needed to and that it was up to the universe to take over. One week later, he contacted me and said he was ready to get started. By maintaining an attitude of patient expectation and detaching from "needing" the client for the money and approval, I let the universe do its work.

As you write your intentions, know that the purpose of all of your intentions is fulfillment and harmony, and that they must be in the best interest of all involved. Sometimes what we think is best is not necessarily what the universe knows is best. For example, since I didn't get the contract with the retail store, I was able to meet many new people and grow myself and my business in a much bigger way. That's why it's important to set your intentions, and then let go and let God.

How to use this book

Creating the big picture

The purpose of this book is to help you create a big, clear picture of who you want to be and what you want to do and have. Clarity is power and knowing where you're going is the first step in getting anywhere. Think about it. When you go on a trip, first you choose your destination and then you map out your journey.

Creating the big picture gives you focus and patience. With no sense of direction, it is too easy to get bogged down with the details of everyday life and give up on what you really want.

When I was a community college instructor, I saw many of my students become overwhelmed by the amount of assignments, homework and tests they had to complete throughout the semester. The ones who didn't have career or personal goals in mind during these stressful times would often give up completely, dropping their classes with only weeks or days left in the semester. The students who had specific career or personal goals completed the tedious tasks with the big picture in mind, thus seeing the light at the end of the tunnel.

Henry David Thoreau said, "If one advances confidently in the direction of his dreams, and endeavors to live the life he has imagined, he will meet with success unexpected in common hours."

It's only possible to get from where you are to where you want to be if you know where you're going. This book is your road map and your intentions are your destinations.

Ask yourself, "If I were to continue down the road I'm on now, where would I end up?" If you're like many people, you either don't know or you don't like your answer!

You have chosen this book because you are ready to live with intention. What do you truly want? What would you attempt if you knew you couldn't fail?

The book

Living with intention requires commitment and dedication. If you are willing and ready to live your best life now, this book is for you. Living with intention is simple and rewarding, but it will only work in your favor through persistence and patient expectancy. This book was written to make the process of living with intention as easy and effortless as possible.

It is divided into ten sections: **Letting Go, Gratitude, Purpose, Abundance, Livelihood, Leisure, Well-being, Relationships, Personal Growth and Legacy.** After working through the first three sections of the book (**Letting Go, Gratitude and Purpose**), you will begin to write your intentions for the seven areas of life.

Intentions for the seven areas of life

Jack Canfield suggests that when setting intentions we divide our lives into seven areas: **Abundance, Livelihood, Leisure, Well-being, Relationships, Personal Growth** and **Legacy.** Since his idea was the starting point for this book, the sections are organized in the same manner.

Each section begins with an inspiring quote, instructions and general affirmations. Then there are blanks for you to fill in with your intentions and space for you to add images (drawings and/or magazine clippings) to better visualize them, so let your imagination take over and your deepest desires come forward.

It is important to be specific and positive, and to write everything in the PRESENT tense, as if it's already yours. It's also a good idea to use –*ing* action verbs and "feeling" words that express how the manifestation of your intentions will make you feel.

For example, write, "I am joyfully earning, saving and investing an income of one million dollars a year by midnight February 25, 2009," instead of "I am rich." Write, "I am happily married to the man of my dreams by June 1, 2015," instead of, "I am not single anymore." Get the idea? If you follow the directions in this book, you will see the manifestation of your intentions.

Use a pencil until you're ready to commit your intentions to pen. As you grow as a person, you will likely grow your intentions. That's perfectly fine! I urge you to keep your intentions in pencil until you feel completely comfortable with your direction.

There's no time limit for completing this book. You can sit down and put it all together in one day, or you can complete it little by little. However you choose to do it, have fun with the process.

Your current results are based on your past thoughts

Getting the results you want in your life starts with your thoughts. You've probably never considered controlling your thoughts; in fact, you have likely spent most of your life letting your thoughts control you.

Living with intention means taking part in the creation of your life through choosing positive and desirable dominant thoughts. By writing down and visualizing the manifestation of your desired thoughts, you will inevitably attract to you your desired results. Remember, that's the Law of Attraction.

The Buddha said, "What we are today comes from our thoughts of yesterday, and our present thoughts build our life of tomorrow: our life is the creation of our mind."

Don't limit your intentions based on your current results; instead, stretch yourself beyond your current results. What do you truly want? What would you attempt if you gave up all of your excuses? If you could be the person you've always wanted to be, what would that look like?

You can be anybody you want to be, have anything you want to have, and do anything you want to do. It's your job to state your intentions, believe in their manifestation and allow your desired results to show up.

Visualize to materialize

Visualization is a very powerful tool in the creative process. In order to intensify the magnetic force of your intentions, visualize them as already in your possession. Whether you realize it or not, you use visualization all the time. For example, when you hear the word house, you don't see the word "house" in your mind. Instead you see a picture of your house. Your mind thinks in pictures, not in words, and having a clear picture of your intentions is one of the best ways to manifest them.

Creating pictures of what you want on the screen of your mind does three things:

- It activates your subconscious mind.

- It opens your reticular activating system (RAS), the filter of your mind, to notice resources that were previously unnoticed.

- It attracts to you people, resources and opportunities to help you reach your goal.

To better visualize your intentions, affix images to represent them after you've written them. If you have a picture of your dream car or house, stick it in the space provided underneath where you write those intentions. You can even draw images if you like. Whatever pictures or symbols you put with your intentions should ignite and strengthen the visualization process for you.

When you read your intentions, be sure to close your eyes for a few moments to visualize them as already complete. Use your imagination and your five senses to see, touch, taste, smell and hear your desired intention. Create a clear picture on the screen of your mind and be sure to visualize the end result.

Commit at least ten minutes a day

Writing your intentions is only the first step to seeing their manifestation. Be sure to read them every morning when you get up, and every night before going to bed visualizing them as already complete. Carry this book with you and read it while you are standing in line at the grocery store, riding the subway or making copies at work. Commit at least ten minutes a day to the process. The more you focus on your intentions, the more you increase your retention of them.

Increasing your level of retention means ingraining your intentions onto the deepest levels of your mind. Retention of your intentions causes dissension, because your current results don't match your desired results. Your mind doesn't like that uncomfortable state of dissension and will go out of its way to make your intention match your reality. That's what manifesting your destiny is all about.

Celebrate your successes and feel good

Your success journal is a good reminder to yourself that the universe is working in your favor, even when you aren't seeing the final results of your intentions. Every day, I write down at least five successes for the day. Some days I even write simple things like "I made the bed."

Writing down my successes has been a very powerful activity. In the past, I would end the day thinking of all the things I hadn't accomplished, thus focusing on lack instead of abundance. Now I know that what I focus on expands, I choose to focus on my successes rather than my failures. The Success Journal at the back of this book gives you a place to make note of your successes along the way. By celebrating each success, you attract more success to you.

Make every effort to feel as good as possible every day. Be positive, energetic and enthusiastic. Since everything is energy, the vibration of your body is truly the beginning of the manifestation of your intentions. Your feelings are a crucial part in the creative process because your feelings determine the vibrational alignment of your body.

Have you ever said, "I get bad vibes from that person"? Or have you ever walked into a room and felt the energy right away, good or bad? That is vibration! The Beach Boys were really on to something when they sang about it in the song "Good Vibrations."

In their book, *The Astonishing Power of Emotions*, Esther and Jerry Hicks explore the role of feelings in the creative process. They declare:

> "It is all about vibrational alignment. Do not look for
> immediate measurable physical results. Instead, look
> for improvement in your mood, your attitude, and
> your emotions. When you feel better, you are more in
> alignment—and everything else will follow."

One emotion that I experience often is "overwhelment." I am the type of person who likes to get everything done my way and on my time. When I feel overwhelmed, my heart rate increases, my muscles tense and I actually get way less done than when I am relaxed. Sound familiar???

Now I understand my emotions are the key to vibrational alignment, which ultimately leads to the physical manifestation of my desires. By releasing overwhelment and with a more relaxed attitude, I allow the flow of life to work through me. Eventually I feel content and relaxed. For example, the title of this book was born out of this process.

I spent many days worrying about what I would call it and forcing the title out of my left-brain. Then one afternoon I decided to lie down, let go and meditate a bit and the title came flooding to me in that relaxed state. Why choose overwhelment when a more optimistic emotion allows better results to come with less effort?

You may feel frustrated at times, but do not let those feelings allow you to lose sight of your goals. Gradually reach for a better feeling emotion. If you find yourself down in the dumps, review the **Letting Go** and **Gratitude** sections of the book or do something to boost your mood, like petting your cat or dog or listening to positive music.

The process of writing and studying this book should be a joyful effort, so if you feel bogged down while working on it, leave it, come back to it later, and in the meantime do something that makes you feel good!

Review of the process of living with intention

- Let go of old programming
- Feel good and remain in a constant state of gratitude
- Live "on purpose"
- Study and visualize your intentions for ten minutes a day, feeling them as already complete
- Believe your intentions are possible
- Detach from outcomes
- Act when appropriate
- Celebrate your successes

One: Letting Go

"The purpose of life is to live it,

to taste experience to the utmost,

to reach out eagerly and without fear

for newer and richer experience."

—Eleanor Roosevelt

One: Letting Go

Letting go is the first step to living with intention and manifesting the life of your dreams. You must throw out all the "I can't" and "I should have" statements in your mind and let old negative energy out in order to let new positive energy in.

You have spent most of your life surrounded by doubt, fear and worry. These toxic emotions will keep you spinning your wheels endlessly, getting you nowhere. You're always going to have some degree of doubt, fear and worry, but endeavoring not to let those emotions stop you is crucial in letting go and being happy.

Did you know that research indicates that you talk to yourself on average 50,000 times per day? Eighty percent of the things that you say to yourself are negative! For example you might say, "I'm never going to get this organized" or "I look fat in these jeans." How much better would you feel if you turned those 80 percent negative thoughts into 80 percent positive ones? Imagine the joy the world would feel if everyone did this!

Think of the news. It is so full of negativity that you can't help but feel depressed. Whether you know it or not, you hold onto that negativity in your subconscious mind. One piece of advice: limit watching and reading the news! Boy, has my life improved by leaps and bounds just from turning off the television!

What is holding you back from living the life you've always wanted for yourself? Is it lack of self-confidence? Is it money and time? Is it training? Is it someone else who doesn't believe in you? Is it the thought of having to do something that is inconvenient? You can be and do anything you desire as long as you don't let excuses get in the way.

Besides doubt, fear and worry, another negative emotion that holds people back is anger. Anger never serves you and is actually toxic to your body. If you have repressed anger about something or somebody from your past that's holding you back, let it go!

When I attended T. Harv Eker's Millionaire Mind Intensive with Chris, I felt as though I had pretty much let go of all doubt, fear, worry and anger that could possibly hold me back from living the life of my dreams. So when we were asked to do a letting-go activity on the last day of the seminar, I wasn't sure I would benefit.

In the activity, we had to write down all of our anger, sadness, fear, guilt and sorrow related to money. The interesting part was that, even though the activity was about money, I found myself writing down many incidences and events that I would have never considered financial in nature. I had no idea that I still had so many negative emotions blocking my way, and most surprisingly of all, built up anger!

After writing down all of our negative feelings at the seminar, we had to choose one especially difficult situation involving another person and anger and relive it with our partner, releasing all of our negativity. It wasn't long before I realized that even though Chris was not the source of my anger, the anger I held onto from the past (which I didn't even know was there) was affecting our healthy relationship!

After we released the negative emotions that were holding us back, we were instructed to write down the other person's side of the story using "I" instead of their first names. We then had to imagine that the person we were angry with was sitting in front of us. We had to listen to their side of the story and forgive them.

We were reminded that there are always two sides to the story and that everyone does the best they can with what they have. Learning to let go of anger and negativity and to forgive is the most difficult, yet most rewarding, choice you'll ever make!

After such a powerful exercise, we quickly replaced our negative emotions with positive ones. This is a very important! You must release negative and replace with positive!

Whether it is anger, fear, worry, doubt or some excuse, be sure to write down on a separate sheet of paper everything that has held you back in the past and could continue to hold you back in the future. If you are having a hard time getting started, think back to times of hurt and pain in your past that you still carry with you.

When you're finished letting go, share the information with someone else (in person or in your thoughts), reliving the negative emotions. Then destroy the paper with the negative thoughts. Shred, burn, or do whatever it takes to consciously tell yourself and the universe that you're ready to start living with intention. Also consider writing the other person's side of the story and forgiving them, either in person or in your thoughts. There is an excellent quote that says, "Holding onto anger and resentment is like drinking poison and expecting someone else to die." *WOW! So true...*

After letting go, be sure to refocus yourself on your positive intentions. Write all the reasons why you no longer feel doubt, fear, worry or anger on the following pages. Focus on all the reasons why you CAN be, do and have anything you desire! Dwelling in the negative only causes more feelings of negativity, while pondering the positive always creates more feelings of joy. After letting go of your toxic emotions and excuses on a separate sheet of paper, complete the following Letting Go pages to re-center yourself. *Restart here...*

Letting Go

I easily and effortlessly let go of all the negative emotions like doubt, fear, worry and anger that hold me back from reaching my goals.

I feel hopeful because…

_____

_____

_____

_____

_____

_____

Letting Go

Nothing can stop me from being the person I want to be or from living the life I deserve.

I feel courageous because…

_____

_____

_____

_____

_____

_____

Letting Go

I believe in myself and my ability to reach my goals.

I feel reassured because…

_____

_____

_____

_____

_____

_____

Letting Go

I know that when I release all negativity and set and believe in my

intentions, that the sky is the limit.

I feel joyful because…

_____

_____

_____

_____

_____

_____

_____

Two: Gratitude

"Be thankful for what you have

and you will end up having more.

But if you concentrate on what you don't have,

you'll never, ever have enough."

—Oprah Winfrey

Two: **Gratitude**

Oprah's advice couldn't be more appropriate for this section. If you spend your time wanting more from life without appreciating what you already have, then you'll never have enough. You must embrace an attitude of gratitude in order to live with intention.

Sometimes it is difficult to be grateful for what you have when you don't feel like you have what you want; however, "scarcity thinking" will only attract more lack. Think abundance and appreciate the person that you are and the person that you are growing to be. Circumstances and people can disappear from your life, but pure inner strength, self-confidence and love can never be taken away.

Be thankful for the little things that you normally take for granted. Bless your ability to read and write in this book. Bless the food you take into your body. Bless your home. Bless your friends, family and pets. Bless the nickel you find on the floor.

Also be grateful for the intentions that you're creating in this book, even before they show up. Rhonda Byrne did this before creating the hit movie, *The Secret.*

"I had no idea how we would bring this knowledge to the screen, but trusted that we would attract the way. I stayed focused and held to the outcome. I felt deep feelings of gratitude in advance. As that became my state of being, the floodgates opened and all the magic flowed into our lives."

Gratitude is an essential part of living with intention. Ever since I became aware of the importance of gratitude, I began to see things from a different perspective and noticed things that I had never noticed before. I take the time to appreciate the shining moon or a singing bird or an interesting cloud. I enjoy the vibrant fall foliage in the North Carolina mountains where I live and admire the perfection of nature. I focus on all of the wonderful people, events and things that bless my life. I am literally blown away at least once a day by something I normally wouldn't have noticed. I also feel gratitude for the promise of a bright future.

Every day before starting work, I say a prayer, which hangs in my office, suggested by Wayne Dyer in his book *Inspiration*. It says, "Thank you God for my life, for my body, for my family and loved ones, for this day and for the opportunity to be of service. Thank you! Thank you! Thank you!" What you focus on expands, so if you focus on what you are grateful for, you attract more to be grateful for into your life.

In this section, list all of the things you are grateful for now. As you go through the book, continue to stay in a state of gratitude and when you think of something new, add it to your list.

If necessary, fill up the backs of the pages as well. Even if your list is not very long right now, make every effort to think of something you're grateful for every day. I can assure you that as you take on an attitude of gratitude, you will see your intentions manifest in your life.

└ yes

Gratitude

I am happy and grateful for…

_____

_____

_____

_____

_____

_____

_____

_____

_____

_____

_____

_____

_____

_____

_____

_____

_____

_____

_____

_____

Gratitude

I am happy and grateful for…

_____

_____

_____

_____

_____

_____

_____

_____

_____

_____

_____

_____

_____

_____

_____

_____

_____

_____

_____

Adair Cates

Gratitude

I am happy and grateful for…

_____

_____

_____

_____

_____

_____

_____

_____

_____

_____

_____

_____

_____

_____

_____

_____

_____

_____

_____

Three: Purpose

"The purpose of life is a life of purpose."

—Robert Byrne

Three: **Purpose**

You're here to serve a unique purpose. Just as writers are born to write and painters are born to paint, you are here to do something great. Because you have had so many people telling you what you should and shouldn't do during your whole life, you have likely lost sight of why you're here. This section will help you rediscover your life purpose.

As I started on my journey of new consciousness, I couldn't help but remember the quote by Robert Byrne as it was ingrained in my head!

When I was younger I loved to read quote books and remember choosing this one when I was about twelve years old to hang on my wall amid award certificates, magazine cut outs of my heartthrobs and pictures of family and friends. It hung there as the centerpiece of all of my dreams.

I have known since I was a child that my purpose was to bring joy to others through my high energy and enthusiasm. After all I am the child who, according to my parents, ran before I walked. I was always on the go and always wanted to be the center of attention. I won speech contests and was awarded the "Most Spirited Cheerleader" trophy at cheerleading camp. I definitely used my energy to my advantage as a child, but over time instead of refocusing my energy in new and exciting ways, I put it away thinking it was inappropriate or immature to be so hyperactive. I always heard, "Chill out!" or "Calm down!", which I took to mean, "Don't be so energetic!"

Recently, I rediscovered that Robert Byrne quote "The purpose of life is a life of purpose" and reclaimed my high energy to do what I love and love what I do! In my office, I have my "Most Spirited Cheerleader" trophy displayed with pride! I now use my enthusiasm in a positive way to inspire and empower others. By putting out high-energy vibrations, I attract the same high energy back to me. I have learned that enthusiasm is an essential element for my success. In fact, the word *enthusiasm* comes from a Greek word that means "the God within us."

The following experience helped me remember another piece of my life purpose: my passion and love for writing. Though I always loved to write, I had never considered writing a book until my husband helped me come up with this book idea. At first I said negative things like, "I'm not patient enough to write a book" or "I don't have enough to say to write a whole book." Well, with a little change of attitude, what you're reading right now came about!

As I began writing this book, I was cleaning out the spare bedroom in our house to make my new office when I came across an old journal. Though I was hurriedly organizing my new space, the little voice in my head said, "Pick up that journal and read it!" I almost rationalized the thought and kept on cleaning, but I knew deep down that there was something to be treasured and learned in this journal. The entry was from April 8, 2002 when I was living in Seville, Spain and teaching English to a very special student Emi. It brought out my life purpose once again!

After so much time wondering what was wrong with me, I finally have figured out that all that needed mending and nurturing was my spirit. I remember the day I realized this. I was having English class with Emi, who I now consider to be the person, the soul who started my journey.

I was telling her that I always had stomachaches. Being a gastroenterologist she told me that all digestive disorders were connected to one's mental state. I thought this sounded a little strange, but then realized that it really did make sense and that all of my recent stomachaches were actually my spirit letting me know it needed to come out, to be revealed and to be developed. Since that conversation, my stomach problems have been minimal.

But that is not really the most important part. Aside from relieving my stomach pains, the revealing of my spirit has caused me to look at the world differently, so I guess you could say that Emi has taught me to look at the world differently. She has taught me how powerful love can be and how one's life can change if he/she does everything for love. She has taught me about our souls, where we go after death, where we come from and why we are the way we are.

She has given me the starting point to take off on my journey and I will use all she has shared with me to build who I am and I will, just as she has done, use my knowledge and experience to change the lives of others. I hope that throughout this journey I remember how important it is to write. Maybe someday I will have enough experience to write my own book.

I will never forget the overwhelming sense of gratitude I felt as I cried after reading this journal entry from five years earlier. I realized that I was doing what I was put on the planet to do by writing this book.

When you're living "on purpose," you work well with the universe and the universe works well with you. You feel good, in harmony and at peace. If you commit to living "on purpose," amazing things will begin to happen. Doors will open, walls will come down and you will attract all the right people into your life.

Once I consciously recommitted to my life purpose—*I live in spirit, peace and abundance and inspire and empower others to do the same*—I felt instantly happier and more fulfilled. I knew that with my purpose I had a starting point for all of my dreams.

My husband is another great example of someone who lives "on purpose." Since he was a young boy, he has loved making music. Growing up, he played and recorded music with his friends and was always in a band. Everything in his life has been focused on his love of music. The times when he has gotten "off purpose," the universe has sent him signs in the form of stomach ulcers and crippling accidents. Chris no longer lets anyone stop him from being who he was put here to be, and that is the reason he is such a success. Visit his website www. chriscates.net to learn more.

Chris and I also created our company Synergy Shift together by melding our life purposes. We do high-energy, fun musical and motivational events for businesses and organizations to inspire and empower others to realize their infinite potential. Check out our website **www.synergyshift.com** for more information. There's nothing better than doing what you love and loving what you do with the love of your life!

Doing what you love and loving what you do is the only way to be truly happy. Take some time to think about what you have to offer the world. What are your strengths and inborn talents? What are you passionate about? Incorporate your answers into an all- encompassing statement.

Think of your life purpose as your personal motto, the "why" of your existence, and thus, your intentions. Quiet your mind by breathing deeply and let the first words that come to you flow onto the paper. Remember, everybody's purpose is to serve others in some way. Go back in your life and remember what you loved as a child and what others loved in you.

If you're having difficulty with this section, I suggest that you go to my website www.adaircates.lifesuccessconsultants.com to download a free MP3 by Bob Proctor called *Purpose, Vision and Goals.* Also, for more clarity, you may want to read the books, *The Life You Were Born to Live*, by Dan Millman and *The Purpose of Your Life*, by Carol Adrienne.

Purpose

What am I passionate about? What do I love doing?

_____

_____

_____

_____

_____

_____

_____

_____

_____

_____

_____

_____

_____

_____

_____

_____

_____

_____

_____

_____

_____

Purpose

What are my strengths and skills? What am I good at?

_____

_____

_____

_____

_____

_____

_____

_____

_____

_____

_____

_____

_____

_____

_____

_____

_____

_____

_____

_____

Purpose

What did I love to do as a child? What memories bring my purpose alive?

_____

_____

_____

_____

_____

_____

_____

_____

_____

_____

_____

_____

_____

_____

_____

_____

_____

_____

Purpose

Who do I want to BE? How can I make a difference?

_____

_____

_____

_____

_____

_____

_____

_____

_____

_____

_____

_____

_____

_____

_____

_____

_____

_____

_____

_____

_____

Purpose

Putting it all together.

My life purpose statement is:

_____

_____

_____

_____

_____

_____

_____

_____

_____

_____

_____

_____

_____

_____

_____

_____

_____

_____

_____

_____

Four: Abundance

"Abundance is not something we acquire.

It is something we tune into."

—Wayne Dyer

Four: Abundance

Have you ever thought about the sheer abundance available on the planet? Think about nature and contemplate her unlimited supply. Think about the grains of sand that make up the beaches, and the salty water that comprises the oceans. Think about the abundance of air, grass and soil on the planet.

There is no shortage in the world other than that which you create in your mind. The universe is infinite and can supply much more than you can ever demand. A rose doesn't demand just a little bit of sunlight!

It is your job through the setting of your intentions to simply ask for what you want. As <u>Bob Proctor</u> reminds us in <u>*The Secret,*</u> it's no accident that 96 percent of the world's wealth is held by one percent of the population. These people know how to tune into abundance consciousness, and now so do you!

In my Master Mind groups, we read the amazing book *Think and Grow Rich* by Napoleon Hill. One of the assignments for the members of the class is to bless money any time they find it. Even if it's a penny or a nickel, instead of looking at it and saying, "Oh. Just another coin," I teach them to say to the universe out loud "Thank you for this symbol of abundance!"

My students soon discovered how remarkable things happen when you take on this attitude of abundance. One of my students Ruby began to bless money any time she found it and got an unexpected check for $1000 in the mail! Another one of my students, initially concerned about having enough money to pay the bills that month, got an unexpected check for just over the necessary amount of money.

I have become a master of blessing money as well. One day I was walking on my street picking up litter as I went and noticed a five-dollar bill on the ground! Boy, did I bless that one!

In this section, write the intentions you have for financial abundance. How much money do you need in order to live your desired lifestyle? What types of material objects do you wish to manifest? If you feel negative about, or undeserving of your abundance intentions, take yourself back to the **Letting Go** section and release any off-putting emotions. Never feel guilty for wanting material possessions, but remember that the true purpose of all your material intentions is to have inner peace, love and harmony.

Write your intentions in the present tense with –*ing* action verbs and "feeling" words. For example, you may write something like, "I am so happily earning, saving and investing $10,000 of passive income every month by July 15, 2010."

Abundance Affirmations

- I am joyfully living in permanent financial freedom.

- I am enjoying a cash flow that allows me to live at my highest potential.

- I am happily managing my money and enjoying financial independence.

- I am earning, saving and investing more than enough money to live my desired lifestyle and to help others.

- I am attracting money easily and effortlessly.

Abundance Intentions

_____

_____

_____

_____

_____

_____

_____

_____

_____

Place images here:

Abundance Intentions

_____

_____

_____

_____

_____

_____

_____

_____

_____

Place images here:

Abundance Intentions

_____

_____

_____

_____

_____

_____

_____

_____

Place images here:

Five: Livelihood

"There is no easy formula for determining

right and wrong livelihood, but it is essential

to keep the question alive.

To return the sense of dignity and honor to manhood,

we have to stop pretending that we can make a

living at something that is trivial or destructive and

still have sense of legitimate self-worth.

A society in which vocation and job are separated

for most people gradually creates an economy

that is often devoid of spirit, one that frequently fills

our pocketbooks at the cost of emptying our souls."

—Sam Keen

Five: Livelihood

Before you complete this section, go back and reread your life purpose statement. This section, probably more than any other, should be a true reflection of your life purpose.

If your current career is not in alignment with your life purpose statement, then maybe one of your intentions in this section will be to try something new. If you feel good about your current career, maybe you just want to improve your sales or your relationship with your boss and/or colleagues. Maybe you want to create some passive streams of income through network marketing or real estate. Maybe you want to retire from your profession in order to pursue a lifelong dream.

Whatever your intentions are they should be focused on what you want to offer the world as compensation. There is no such thing as something for nothing.

Think about a current product or service you offer that you would like to improve upon, or set your intention on something entirely new.

Right before I finished writing this book, I had a huge change in livelihood. I decided to quit my teaching job in order to pursue a career as a motivational speaker, trainer, coach and author. Though it was liberating to leave behind a job that was no longer fulfilling to me, it was also imperative that I intend to offer the world something as compensation. I aligned with my life purpose statement and began taking action by writing this book, attending networking events, signing up for two trainings and joining Toastmasters. Remember, the energy you put out is the energy you get back. There truly is no such thing as something for nothing.

Go back and read the Sam Keen quote at the beginning of this section and know that your days of earning wages for the betterment of someone else's business are ending and the days of working for true self-fulfillment are here. In order to reach your true potential in your life, you must be someone and do something you believe in.

Write what you intend to create in the context of livelihood. What product or service do you intend to offer, and at what price? For example, you may write, "I am joyfully running my own Internet business out of my home office and earn $5,000 a month by November 22, 2012." Remember to be positive, to push your current limits and to intend the livelihood that you deserve.

Livelihood Affirmations

• I am blissfully living out my life purpose.

• I am cheerfully making money by adding value to
other people's lives.

• I am gladly working less and less and making more
and more money.

• All work that I engage in is joyful effort. My vocation
is my vacation.

• I am doing what I love and loving what I do.

Livelihood Intentions

_____

_____

_____

_____

_____

_____

_____

_____

_____

Place images here:

Livelihood Intentions

_____

_____

_____

_____

_____

_____

_____

_____

Place images here:

Livelihood Intentions

_____

_____

_____

_____

_____

_____

_____

_____

_____

Place images here:

Six: Leisure

"The wisdom of a learned man

cometh by opportunity of leisure:

and he that hath little business shall become wise."

—Ecclesiastes 24

Six: Leisure

What do you think of when you think of leisure? I think of doing something I love, with no concerns about time or money. For me, leisure is about feeling good, relaxing and celebrating fun. One of my goals is to make some time for leisure every day, whether by playing nine holes of golf with my husband or sitting on the back patio reading a book for an hour. Taking time for leisure means getting away from the hustle and bustle of everyday life and doing something that makes you smile!

Leisure is probably something you never have an abundance of, so in this section take some time to daydream and ask yourself all the "w" questions about your free time: WHO do you want to spend it with? WHAT do you want to do? WHEN do you want to do it? WHERE do you want to be?

Most of us can think about the leisurely lifestyle we would like to live but quickly limit ourselves with constraints like money and time. So if you had no constraints whatsoever, how would you spend your free time? What would you do for fun?

Never base these or any other intentions in this book on your current situation. You're trying to break your old ways, not perpetuate them!

Your intention may be to play golf five times a week with your spouse at the country club in your hometown. Or maybe it's to spend a month every year at your second home on the beach.

Whatever it is, make sure it focuses on the "what," not the "how," and to write it as if it's already yours. For example, "I am lazily floating around my salt-water pool in my backyard while my kids are playing around me by July 4, 2012."

Leisure Affirmations

- I am gleefully living a life of leisure and luxury.

- I am vacationing in the most beautiful places
  in the world.

- I am enjoying lots of free time with family
  and friends.

- I am lightheartedly having fun every day.

Leisure Intentions

_____

_____

_____

_____

_____

_____

_____

_____

_____

Place images here:

Leisure Intentions

_____

_____

_____

_____

_____

_____

_____

_____

_____

Place images here:

Leisure Intentions

_____

_____

_____

_____

_____

_____

_____

_____

Place images here:

Seven: Well-being

"The secret of health for both mind and body

is not to mourn for the past,

worry about the future,

or anticipate troubles,

but to live in the present moment

wisely and earnestly."

—Buddha

Seven: Well-being

Undoubtedly, you understand the importance of good health. If you don't have your health, what do you have?

Remember the journal entry I found when I rediscovered my life purpose? My almost chronic stomachaches went away when I began to live from my heart and reveal my spirit. It was life-changing for me to realize that my physical condition was a culmination of mental, emotional and spiritual stress.

There have been other times in my life when I had all sorts of disrupting ailments as well. One of the worst was when I had constant tingling in my right arm and leg. I went through all sorts of appointments and tests before being told that nothing was wrong with me. I remember being so frustrated because I wanted an explanation as to why I was feeling that way. Then someone said to me, "The body has an interesting way of telling us that we have too much stress in our lives."

At the time I didn't think I was stressed, but now looking back, I know that I was. I was working full time as a teacher and pursuing my Masters degree. I had very little time for relaxing. Only when I began to take care of myself emotionally, mentally and spiritually did my tingling subside.

When you think of health, you probably think mostly about physical well-being; however, science is revealing more and more that physical health is merely a printout of emotional, mental and spiritual health. In other words, the physical aspect of health is the culmination of what's going on in the invisible world of emotions, thoughts and spirit.

Your body, in combination with the foods you eat, contains everything you need to stay in perfect harmony and balance. If you choose to take good care of your physical body by exercising, eating right, and staying free of toxins, and you remain at peace emotionally, mentally and spiritually, you will be in a state of well being.

In this section, write down your intentions for good health. What kind of diet do you want to eat? What kind of shape do you want to be in? How do you want to feel on a daily basis? Whether you wish to maintain your good health or are endeavoring to improve it, your well-being is foundational to your success in all areas of your life

Well-being Affirmations

- I am gracefully living in my in-shape, healthy
  and energetic body.

- I am perfection in human form and remain
  free of disease.

- I am joyfully feeling wonderful on the inside and out.

- I take care of myself by eating healthfully and
  drinking lots of water.

Adair Cates

Well-being Intentions

_____

_____

_____

_____

_____

_____

_____

_____

_____

Place images here:

Well-being Intentions

_____

_____

_____

_____

_____

_____

_____

_____

Place images here:

Well-being Intentions

_____

_____

_____

_____

_____

_____

_____

_____

_____

Place images here:

Eight: Relationships

"Undoubtedly to some, the idea

of giving so much love to self will

seem very cold, hard and unmerciful.

Still this matter may be seen in a different light,

when we find that 'looking out for Number One,'

as directed by the Infinite,

is really looking out for Number Two

and is indeed the only way

to permanently benefit Number Two."

—Prentice Mulford

Eight: Relationships

Just as Mulford says, you must first have a good relationship with yourself before you can have a good relationship with others. By completing this book, you are proving to yourself and the universe that you care enough to invest in the creation of your life. Continue to have self-confidence and self-respect and you will attract quality relationships.

There is no better way to get more love in your life than to love yourself. When you feel good about yourself, that good feeling is emitted to the universe, and therefore, because of the powerful Law of Attraction, that is what you will get back.

We don't live alone in a bubble so we must endeavor to make every effort to be in harmony with the people around us. This can be challenging sometimes because every individual is full of unique thoughts, beliefs, feelings and ideas, some of which may not resonate with you.

Your job on the planet is to cooperate and to create positive synergy with others, not to convince others that their beliefs are wrong and yours are right. I love what T. Harv Eker says, "You can be right, or you can be happy." Living with intention is not about competing, but about creating.

One invaluable element of good relationships is the importance of being present. I learned this from Brian Biro, a world-class motivational trainer and author of *Beyond Success*. He points out in his book and seminars that most people are not fully in the present moment. Brian shares a touching story about how not being present with his young daughters brought about his commitment to be a father and a husband above all else. Choosing to be present is crucial to living with intention. Make an effort to be a good listener and to be more inter-est*ed* than interest*ing*.

As a teacher, I learned the hard way the importance of being present for my students. When I first started teaching, I was very focused on lesson plans, attendance and grades. I forgot that the whole reason I was there was to teach and learn from my students. Because of this, my first year and a half of teaching was very difficult and stressful. As soon as I took the focus off of myself and the secondary tasks involved in teaching, I became more present and my job was way more rewarding.

I learned that in order to hold my students' interest and help them succeed in the classroom that I had to have good relationships with them as individuals. On my last day of class after resigning from my position at the community college where I taught, I was flooded with cards and gifts of gratitude from my students that I know I would have never gotten had I not been a teacher who truly cared and was present for her students.

One of my students wrote in a card:

> *I was shocked when I found out I had a teacher who sincerely cared about what was going on in my life. That was shocking, but AWESOME. You would take not only a few minutes to talk to me or other students about situations but often times a lot of time out of your busy day. I think it is amazing how you talk to and try to help people who in my opinion have very difficult personalities. Yes I noticed! Other teachers just assume that students don't have an interest in talking about their problems, but you took time to dig into their interests and goals and to help them strive to meet them.*

Human relationships enhance our lives far beyond our individual attempts at happiness. Good relationships create meaning and bring out the best in us. Be present for others and you will be infinitely rewarded. Whether it's someone you talk to in passing at the grocery store or your spouse, remember the importance of being present as you set intentions for your relationships.

Think of the intentions you would like to set in order to have great relationships with your spouse, family members, friends, co-workers and even strangers. For example, you might write, "I am amazingly and effortlessly feeling confident at work and maintaining a harmonious relationship with my boss and co-workers by January 5, 2009." Keep all of your relationship intentions in rapport with the relationship that you aim to have with yourself.

Relationships Affirmations

- I am present for others.

- I am cheerfully interacting with family, friends
  and everyone I encounter.

- I am always striving to do what is best for all involved.

- I am lovingly reaching out to others and am
  open to receiving their love in return.

- I am living from my heart.

Adair Cates

Relationship Intentions

_____

_____

_____

_____

_____

_____ .

_____

_____

_____

Place images here:

Relationship Intentions

_____

_____

_____

_____

_____

_____

_____

_____

_____

Place images here:

Relationship Intentions

_____

_____

_____

_____

_____

_____

_____

_____

Place images here:

Nine: Personal Growth

"Believe in yourself and all that you are.
Know that there is something inside you
that is greater than any obstacle."

—Christian D. Larson

Adair Cates

Nine: **Personal Growth**

Have you ever heard the saying, "If you're not growing, you're dying?" What an amazing truth! You're obviously choosing to grow if you are reading and writing in this book, so in this section, write your intentions on how you can continue to grow as an individual.

Write down any special talents or activities that you want to improve or learn in order to push yourself away from your comfort zone and into your growth zone.

Maybe you want to run a marathon or learn how to scuba dive (a couple of my personal growth intentions). Maybe you have always wanted to learn how to play the piano or speed-read. Maybe you want to go back to school to earn a degree. Whatever it may be, make sure it is something that intrigues you enough to hold your interest and challenges you enough to keep you growing.

When you push yourself to new limits, your mind will begin to play tricks on you. You'll begin telling yourself that there's no way you can do this or that, and you'll discourage your growth. Push past your false limitations and reach for something new and exciting. When that little voice inside your head says, "You can't possibly do that," reply back with "Thank you for sharing," and replace that negative chatter with something positive and assuring. You can also do this with people who discourage you from going after your dreams. The sky's the limit! If you want to feel successful and joyous, you have to challenge yourself to reach new levels.

At one point in my past, my mind was telling me that I couldn't write a book; however, I kept believing in myself and thinking about how awesome it would feel to hold my first book in my hands. I felt gratitude for the outcome and moved confidently in the direction of my dream.

I have friends who have run marathons who never thought it possible to run 26.2 miles. They started with the first step on the first day of training and pushed themselves through to the finish line of the race, not really knowing how they were going to do it but doing it anyway.

As Martin Luther King Jr, said, "You don't have to see the whole staircase, just take the first step." It's critical to take action towards what you want one step at a time.

One of my personal growth intentions is, "I am singing with a beautiful and unique voice onstage with my husband, Chris, in front of an audience of a thousand people by May 12, 2009." Time to get started on those voice lessons! Ready, fire, aim!

Personal Growth Affirmations

- I am blissfully stretching my limits and learning new and exciting things every day.

- I am proving to myself more and more that I can do anything I put my mind to.

- I am happily co-creating my life by trying new things and never giving up.

- I am learning to trust my higher self to guide me to do the things that mean the most.

Personal Growth Intentions

_____

_____

_____

_____

_____

_____

_____

_____

Place images here:

Personal Growth Intentions

_____

_____

_____

_____

_____

_____

_____

_____

Place images here:

Personal Growth Intentions

_____

_____

_____

_____

_____

_____

_____

_____

_____

Place images here:

Adair Cates

Ten: Legacy

"There are certain things that are fundamental to human fulfillment.

The essence of these needs is captured in the phrase

'to live, to love, to learn, to leave a legacy'.

The need to live is our physical need for such things as food,

clothing, shelter, economical well being, health.

The need to love is our social need to relate to other people,

to belong, to love and to be loved.

The need to learn is our mental need to develop and to grow.

And the need to leave a legacy is our spiritual need to have a sense of

meaning, purpose, personal congruence, and contribution"

—Stephen R. Covey

Ten: Legacy

Everybody wants to make a difference in the world. Teachers want to positively affect their students, parents want to inspire their children and environmentalists want to improve the state of our planet.

Whether you realize it or not, you are leaving footprints every day as you journey through life. Your legacy can only grow to the extent that you do.

How do you treat others? How do you live every day in service? How do you radiate joy, love and passion in even the most mundane of tasks?

You have probably heard the story of the little girl on the beach who one by one picks up the starfish and throws them back into the sea before the hot sun dries them out. A man approaches the girl and tells her that there are so many starfish to throw back she can't possibly make a difference. As she throws the next starfish back to its home, she replies, "It made a difference to that one."

You touch the lives of all of those you meet by being an example. Ralph Waldo Emerson said, "What you do speaks so loudly that I can't hear what you say." Strive to be the best you can be in all situations.

Think of what you can do to leave a positive legacy. What is your contribution? How do you make the world a better place? For example, you may write, "I am easily and effortlessly contributing at least 10 percent of my income to the charity of my choice by July 7, 2009."

One of my intentions for this section is to start my own charity that will allow people with limited incomes to attend personal growth seminars and conferences.

Legacy Affirmations

- I am gleefully feeling gratitude for all in my life and for all that is to come.

- I am excitedly giving to those who are in need.

- I am blissfully learning and teaching every day to help myself and others grow.

- I always give 100 percent and do my best at all times.

- I am openly accepting new and different experiences and people.

- I am making the world a better place.

Adair Cates

Legacy Intentions

_____

_____

_____

_____

_____

_____

_____

_____

_____

Place images here:

Legacy Intentions

_____

_____

_____

_____

_____

_____

_____

_____

_____

Place images here:

Legacy Intentions

_____

_____

_____

_____

_____

_____

_____

_____

_____

Place images here:

Your Journey Starts Here!

Congratulations on finishing this book! I hope you have enjoyed the process and are learning more about yourself every day. Though this is the end of the book, it is truly the beginning of your creative journey.

I urge you to study your intentions for at least ten minutes a day, and as you meet with success, no matter how small it may seem, celebrate and write about it in the Success Journal at the back of the book. Continue to grow and be open and willing to do what it takes to see your intentions through to manifestation.

As you are reading and visualizing your intentions, remember another powerful universal law, The Law of Gender, which states that everything has a gestation period. Just because you aren't seeing the results you want in the physical world doesn't mean that your intentions aren't manifesting. Ninety-nine percent of who we are is invisible!

When you live as the master of your life and work in harmony with humanity and the universe, everything will come full circle.

Stay true to your purpose, and act. Action is the bridge between the physical world of results and the nonphysical world of thought. Hold tight to your vision and know that anything is possible.

As you continue on your journey of conscious creation, if you feel the need to chunk down you intentions into smaller action steps, create a goal notebook for yourself. Write your big intention at the top of one page and list underneath it specific action steps that you can take to bring yourself closer to the completion of your intention. Remember, the journey is never over! Once you accomplish your intentions, start the process all over again! Life is a fascinating journey of constant growth and expansion.

I BELIEVE in YOU!

As William Ernest Henley said, "You are the master of your own fate. The captain of your own soul." So sail your ship confidently in the direction of your dreams. Have faith and live with intention! Best wishes!

Live with Intention

Success Journal

"Success is a journey, not a destination."

—**Ben Sweetland**

Adair Cates

Success Journal

_____

_____

_____

_____

_____

_____

_____

_____

_____

_____

_____

_____

_____

_____

_____

_____

_____

_____

_____

_____

Success Journal

_____

_____

_____

_____

_____

_____

_____

_____

_____

_____

_____

_____

_____

_____

_____

_____

_____

_____

_____

_____

_____

_____

Success Journal

_____

_____

_____

_____

_____

_____

_____

_____

_____

_____

_____

_____

_____

_____

_____

_____

_____

_____

_____

_____

_____

Resources

The Success Principles, by Jack Canfield. New York: HarperCollins, 2005

The Secret, by Rhonda Byrne. New York: Atria, 2006

The Power of Intention, by Dr. Wayne W. Dyer. Carlsbad, CA: Hay House, 2004

Inspiration, by Dr. Wayne W. Dyer. Carlsbad, CA: Hay House, 2006

The Attractor Factor, by Joe Vitale. Hoboken, NJ: John Wiley and Sons, 2005

The Spontaneous Fulfillment of Desire, by Deepak Chopra. New York: Three Rivers Press, 2003

Beyond Success, by Brian Biro. New York: Perigee, 2001

Secrets of the Millionaire Mind, by T. Harv Eker. New York: Harper-Collins, 2005

The Life Your Were Born to Live, by Dan Millman. Tiburon, CA: HJ Kramer, 1993

The Purpose of Your Life, by Carol Adrienne. New York: Eagle Brook, 1998

Think and Grow Rich: The Original Version Restored and Revised, by Napoleon Hill. San Diego, CA: Aventine Press, 2004

The Astonishing Power of Emotions, by Esther and Jerry Hicks. Carlsbad, CA: Hay House, 2007

Adair Cates

About the Author

Adair Cates lives with intention, passion and purpose and believes that now is the time to break free from doubt, fear and worry and start living the life of your dreams. With her vibrant and joyful personality, she captivates you to see something inside of yourself that you've never noticed before. She'll make you laugh, cry and open your eyes to a whole new world of possibility with her astonishing ability to motivate people from all walks of life.

Before beginning her career as a motivational speaker and coach, Adair taught Spanish in middle school and community college for five years. While helping her students become conscious of the opportunities available to them, Adair herself had an awakening. She realized that what she loved most about teaching was helping her students to recognize and reach their true potential.

No longer feeling fulfilled teaching grammar and vocabulary, she took a leap of faith and followed her heart in pursuit of her goal. She felt she was born to help others discover their life purpose and to create their highest vision. Knowing there is an abundance of love, harmony and prosperity available for everyone, Adair inspires and empowers others to go after their dreams and to create a life full of bliss and inspiration.

Adair focuses on people's ability to go within to manifest their desires. She believes that success is a choice that is available to all who accept it. Getting from where you are to where you want to be isn't about pushing and working hard to achieve, but about going with the flow and intending and allowing the right people and events to come into your life. Adair is committed to helping others through her true, heartfelt purpose. She focuses on the positive energy that flows through every living being on the planet and knows that everything happens for a reason.

Adair resides in Asheville, NC with her husband, musician Chris Cates and their two cats, Lionel and Wario. She and Chris work together in their company Synergy Shift performing dynamic, high-energy musical and motivational events around the globe. For more information go to their website at **www.synergyshift.com**.

Would you like some additional encouragement and support while working through *Live With Intention*? Contact Adair Cates at adair@synergyshift.com to set up a FREE thirty-minute phone consultation.

To hear Chris Cates' music and download a FREE song, visit www.synergyshift.com.

Adair Cates also:
- Tailors corporate events
- Conducts Tele-Seminars
- Conducts live Seminars
- Coaches individuals and groups
- Produces a monthly newsletter—sign up for FREE at www.synergyshift.com.

For additional products and services by Synergy Shift, visit www.synergyshift.com or call 828-413-4019.

Contact the Cates' today to book a fun, uplifting musical and motivational event for your business or organization. Their events are perfect for sales teams, network marketing groups, non-profits and schools.

This book will be available soon in Spanish, along with other resources. Adair is available to do her talks in Spanish.

6853857R00105

Made in the USA
San Bernardino, CA
16 December 2013